Under the Sea

Edited by Gillian Doherty
With thanks to Dr. Margaret Rostron and
Dr. John Rostron for information about sea life.

This edition published in 2011 by Usborne Publishing Ltd, 83-85 Saffron Hill, London EC1N 8RT, England.
www.usborne.com Copyright © 2011, 2007 Usborne Publishing Ltd. The name Usborne and the
devices ♀☺ are Trade Marks of Usborne Publishing Ltd. All rights reserved. No part of this
publication may be reproduced, stored in a retrieval system, or transmitted in any form or
by any means, electronic, mechanical, photocopying, recording or otherwise,
without prior permission of the publisher. UE. Printed in Dubai.

Under the Sea

Anna Milbourne

Illustrated by Cathy Shimmen

Designed by Nicola Butler

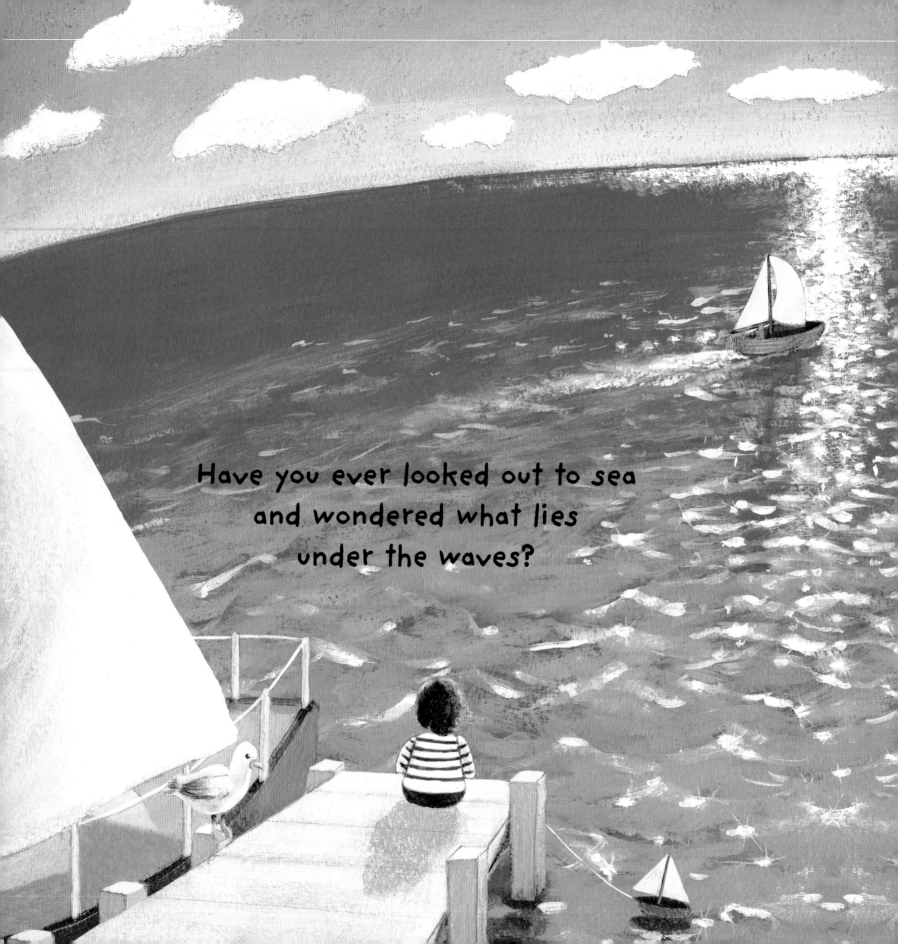

Have you ever looked out to sea
and wondered what lies
under the waves?

The sea is so big it reaches all around the world.
In each place it's as different as can be.

Near a sunny shore, where the water is warm, there are hundreds of jewel-bright fish.

They bustle around the coral reef nibbling at teeny-tiny plants.

A turtle swims along
and settles on the seabed...

where lots of eager, yellow fish
crowd around to clean its shell.

At night, the fish tuck themselves
into nooks and crannies to go to sleep.

A hungry eel slinks out
of its hole to hunt.

Any creature it finds
might become a midnight snack!

When morning comes, the eel skulks home,
and other creatures roam around.

In an underwater meadow,
sea cows munch on long sea grass.

A group of rays
swims slowly by.

They flap their wings as though they're flying
and glide out into the open sea.

Imagine sailing across the wide, blue sea.
There's nothing but water for miles and miles.

Then suddenly beneath you swims
the **biggest** creature there's ever been.

It's a gentle giant — a big blue whale.
He's searching for other whales.

He sings a booming, lonely song
into the empty blue.

From far away across the sea,
another whale's song comes floating back.

Out here, far from any shore, the sea is VERY deep.

It gets darker and darker
the deeper you go.

Then, all at once,
twinkling lights appear.

All kinds of strange and pretty creatures are flashing messages in the dark.

It takes hours to get
to the bottom of the sea.

People have been there
in little submarines.

They found mountains and valleys,
just like you see on land.

But there were other things
no one had ever seen before.

Odd, rocky chimneys
puff out hot, black water...

and pearly crabs
and scarlet tubeworms
live all around.

Not many things live at the bottom of the sea.
Most live near the top, where it's sparkling-bright.

Tumbling schools of silvery fish rush along beneath the waves.

Dolphins chase after them,
rounding up the fish to eat.

Dolphins can't breathe underwater
like all the fishes do.

They have to breathe the air instead,
through little blowholes on their heads.

They leap out of the water as they speed along,
and catch a breath before they dive back down.

You could spend forever and a day
exploring the deep, blue sea.

But sail far enough across the waves
and you'll always come to shore.